RECURRING

REVENUE

A Practical guide to help you launch your very own *Software-as-a-service* business

FRANK DAPPAH

Copyright © 2019 Ostrich Publishers

All rights reserved.

ISBN: 9781077129801

AUTHOR'S NOTE
ACCIDENTAL SUCCESS

We (My wife and I, our employees, the company) found our way into the tech world, specifically, the world of software services as a result of a confluence of positive, but unlikely events.
We were looking for a new software vendor for our insurance business. The company we were associated with had made a change to their product. A change that meant that they no longer provided a service offering that met our business needs.

During our search, we discovered that there was a limited number of companies who provided the type of service we were looking for. The truth is, there were many vendors who provided the service we required, in a general sense, but none had the specific features we required. We figured; we cannot be the only insurance agency having this issue. We did some research and found out that there were many firms out in the marketplace looking for the kind of features we required, but very few companies who met that need.

Was this a golden opportunity? Could we build a software application for ourselves, and perhaps, others? How would we even go about this? Keep in mind, I am not a software engineer, but I do have some graphic design chops and very little HTML coding skills. I embarked on a mission to find a software developer to build the app we needed. I found this person in Rajib, the coder who would become my friend and business partner and would help us build a six-figure software business.

CONTENTS

CHAPTER ONE   **Plan it**

Brainstorming	2
Anatomy of a "Good" Idea	4
Think Outside the box	9

CHAPTER TWO   **Build it**

We can't all write code	21
Finding a Developer	22
Marketing and the big picture	28
Design your Beta With your Audience in mind	41
Pricing models	47
Beta Testing	68

CHAPTER THREE   **Sell it**

Ways to market your new SaaS App	81
Facebook Ads Work	94
It's a Saas life for me	113

Dedicated to Bernice

RECURRING REVENUE

A Practical guide to help you launch your very own *Software-as-a-service* business

FRANK DAPPAH

CHAPTER ONE

PLAN IT

Brainstorming

I get tons of emails a day from Entrepreneurs just like you. Often times, these are just folks looking to share a tip about some new business software application.

Sometimes, I am asked about my opinions about small business trends and/ or some phenomenon in the marketplace. Out of the hundreds of questions I get a month, the one often asked, in one form or another is "**What is a good business idea?**". Of course, "good", in this context means, Profitable, Scalable, etc.

I am sure you will agree that you never know if your business idea will ultimately be the next big thing, or just a dud till you build it, create it and put it out there to see how the market reacts to it.

There are some steps, however that one can take to try to gauge the viability of any business idea. In this chapter, we shall look at ways to test the market fitness of any software product idea you may have.

Natural Market VS Foreign Concept

There are various advantages to starting a software business or launching a new software application to meet the needs of an industry you are already familiar with, a market that you are in or have some prior experience.

If this describes your situation, then know that you are in an awesome position to build a product that will directly address the needs, wants, pain points of folks in that market. You have been there and therefore; you know their pain and what kind of tool will make their lives easier. Remember, you are one of them.

On the other hand, if you are thinking about building a tool for a business or industry you have had no experience in, then you will want to spend more time doing your due diligence, research and market analysis.

There are various tools out there, I have discovered, that will help you test out your idea and gauge the market need for such a tool before you commit time and money to creating it

Anatomy of a "Good" Idea

So, what is a good idea for a Software-As-A-Service product? What does a good SAAS idea look like? Well, the answer, as they say, is complicated. That being said, let's start with the basics. In my opinion, any viable business idea, regardless of which industry you are looking to get into, should have these three components:

Solves a problem - Will your product solve a major headache in your market. If you are building your SAAS platform to serve other businesses, will they be able to do their jobs better with your product?

For consumers, will your app make their lives easier, as in provide some sort of convenience and relieve a major pain point in their daily activities?

Unique-With billions of apps out there, and new ones being built every day, this quality of the app is of course getting harder to distinguish. However, your idea must have some unique quality in features or the way it will be positioned to users. In other words, what will make users pick your platform over other similar ones.

Sizable Market - Are there enough potential users out there to justify putting time and money into building your software application? Now, I will be the first to admit that one man's or woman sizable market is another's "Not worth building". Of course, whether you think the potential user base for a product is big enough will depend on your needs and plans.

Even better if...

No two business ideas are the same. Some ideas require a lot of upfront investment capital, not to mention months, even years of research and development to bring it to market. While others need very little initial effort. Note that neither route predicts guaranteed success.

That being said, based on my years of experience launching three successful businesses and dozens of software applications, I believe you, as an entrepreneur stand a greater chance of success if you can identify some of these traits in your new idea.

Area of expertise- Like I mentioned earlier and cannot stress enough. Your new SAAS idea stands a much better chance at success if built for a market in which you have significant experience. Something to do with your current or past job role.

This way you will be very familiar with which features someone in that position will value the most. You will be able to speak the language of the industry, which will go a long way when marketing your new product to potential users.

Low Startup cost- The great thing about globalization and the internet is that you can work with software engineers from all over the world. Gone are the days when one had to pony up thousands of dollars just to build a prototype of their software tool.

These days, you can significantly reduce your startup cost in any business by outsourcing some or all of the initial coding to folks in other countries. I recommend that you try to find SAAS ideas that require minimal upfront cost.

Ongoing need - This is a no brainer; If you wish to build a software tool that will provide recurring revenue, then you will have to devote your resources to building a tool that your customers will need to use on an ongoing basis and regularly.

For example, Netflix can keep charging your Credit card on a monthly basis, and you be ok with it because you watch TV often. However, If you use a service once, to unlock your car after you leaving your keys in it, you would not be ok with having the service provider charge you on a monthly basis, for the same service, since locking yourself out of your car isn't something that happens often.

Scalability - This quality is one I personally always look for in any product or business idea I look at. Can you scale your idea with very little need to build up a large staff or sales team? I call this the "One-to-many" feature. Where your sell one product to many users over and over. This is actually the most attractive thing about the Software-as-a-Service business, to me at least.

Thanks to the internet and tools like Zendesk, you can build a product that will be used by hundreds, thousands, even millions of people without the need to hire a bunch of customer service and sales folks. Your users can go online, signup and pay without having to contact you. They can find all the answers they need about your product on your website or via your self-help portal.

Moat- This is actually a concept I borrowed from the Greatest Investor of our time, Warren Buffett. Buffet uses this principle to select the business he decides to invest in, and that is, they must have a Moat. As in a "Moat" around the castle to keep invaders out.

Does your idea have this quality? Do you have some kind of special skill or Intellectual property you plan to use to build or deliver your product to market? Something that will make it difficult for your competitors or any potential invaders to replicate and eventually steal your lunch?

Think Outside the box

At this time, I thought I would share some insights

on how to create a unique product and generate sales using the power of human behavior. These are some unusual ideas I am going to share with you, so bear with me.

Would you agree that The National Enquirer, the now infamous tabloid and other similar products wouldn't be able to sell a single copy of their magazines to grocery shoppers weren't for the fact that they place copies of their product, almost exclusively by the cash register?

We can even expand this thought process beyond salacious tabloids and apply this concept to all the knickknacks and candy bars that we see during our checkout at our local grocery store. These companies are all taking advantage of one common human behavior: Our fear of being bored.

We humans, even more so these days, with social media and smartphones, dread not having anything to do, at any time during the day.

We really hate being bored...

Various academic studies, including one conducted by Psychologists at the University of Virginia and Harvard found that among our many fears, one surprising phobia is being left alone with our thoughts. During the study, the researchers found that people would rather do anything, than do nothing for any period of time, including causing physical pain to themselves in order to pass the time.

The study featured 30 men and women of ages 18 to 77. The subjects of the study were told to sit alone for 15 minutes away from their mobile devices, Televisions, and any other distractions. Most participants did not enjoy the solitude and some even felt the time spent alone was far longer than it actually was.

The Researchers were further surprised to learn that

67% of the men and 25% of the women in the study were willing to administer an electric shock to themselves to avoid being bored.

As an Aspiring SAAS Entrepreneur, you must devote some time to delve into human behavior. Especially if you are planning to build a software application with consumers as your core audience. Note that businesses will typically choose a product based on whether or not it helps achieve the overall goals of the company.

Consumers, on the other hand base most of their daily purchases, including which subscription services they use based on a complex mix of motives, with emotions as a main factor.

We take expensive vacations, these days, not because we need a break from the monotony of our daily grind, but because our friends have been to Maui recently and they have thousands of photos on social media to prove it, and we will be damned if we let them outdo us. We rush to the theaters, not to check out the latest blockbuster but because all our friends are talking about it on Twitter, and we pretend we loved the movie only because everyone in our social circle say they did.

Think of all the predictive signs of human behavior to use as tools to attracts users to your products. Like the fear of missing out (FOMO), especially when marketing to younger audiences, the need to attain social status, the desire to constantly voice our opinions, and many more.

Conclusion: Points to Remember

At this time, I think it's worth going over the most important points shared in the first chapter of this book. Building a software business, or any business for that matter, is a process. There are no cheat codes or hacks. None that I am aware of at least. Not any that I have witnessed, based on my experience as an entrepreneur. The success or failure of your SAAS business will greatly depend on the amount of time and effort you put into the planning portion of this process.

Planning is Key

"Give me six hours to chop down a tree and I will spend the first four sharpening the axe."
— Abraham Lincoln

Do not leave anything to chance. Plan out your product features carefully. Think thoroughly about your potential users' needs and wants. Carefully put together a multifaceted sales and marketing strategy. One that directly communicates your value proposition in a way that will have an impact on your intended audience.

Form alliances

""Talent wins games, but teamwork and intelligence win championships."
— Michael Jordan

Consider forming strategic partnerships with others. Those that are equipped with the skills and resources to help further your goals. Success is truly a team sport and you should not be afraid to find those that share your ambitions and have the tools you do not have to help. You might also want to, depending on the cost, get a beta version of your app completed, and to find a handful of Angel investors to help cover the cost of initial production.

With that being said, as you continue to read this book, consider the following points:

Build for a Natural market

When building a Software product to market to other businesses, and even to a lesser extent, consumers, you stand a greater chance at success when you target an industry, you're familiar with and have some prior experience in.

Customer profiling

During the brainstorming / planning phase for your app It helps to analyze the demographics and behavior of typical target customer, build your application with your potential users' wants, needs, lifestyles, etc. In mind.

Anatomy of a "Good" idea

Any viable idea for a software product, or any product for that matter, should solve an annoying enough problem, have a large potential user base, and should be unique. Uniqueness, however, comes in many different forms. Set your product apart from the rest.

"V" is for Value

The key to creating a software app, that is sure to gain market share, and build a large user base is value. Regardless of how great your marketing campaign is, or which experts worked on your project, and how much you spend on flashy ads; you will have a very hard time attracting and retaining users if your platform doesn't deliver on the "Value" side of the equation. Folks need to get something out of using your app. Here, we are talking about the "What's in it for me" factor.

I could write a whole book on this very topic. Most entrepreneurs do not pay enough attention to this particular point, causing them to build apps that only resonates with them and not the end user. I want you to position yourself and your company to "Win". I, therefore, need you to obsess over creating a product that meets the unique needs and wants of your typical user.

Keep improving on the user experience. Keep adding features that are built specifically for your users and their evolving expectations. Collect as much feedback from your customers as possible. Use this feedback to create features, that add more value to your product. Do not be afraid to spell out these value-adding features when marketing your product.

CHAPTER TWO

BUILD IT

We can't all write code

Now that you have nailed down the idea and concept for your SaaS platform, it is time to start building your app. Thing is, most software entrepreneurs are typically software developers themselves, or, at the very least do have some coding skills.

Most can build basic applications. If you are one who can code yourself, then the next section will definitely not apply to you. But if you are just like me and have zero coding skills, well, except some basic HTML knowledge, then it is time to find yourself a developer to work with.

In the next section I will provide some resources and tips to consider when looking for a software developer to help bring your ideas to life. These tips are one hundred percent based on my personal experiences.

Finding a Developer

Finding a developer to help you build your software application will, without a doubt, be the most consequential step you take during the entire process of building your app. and business.

For the sake of sticking to a restrictive budget while getting a quality product, you will get the most bang for your buck if you think on a global level. You will be able to find quality professionals from places like India, Pakistan, Lebanon, and Israel.

In the past, I have worked well and completed many projects working with folks from these countries. Remember, we are all, whether you like it or not, living in a global world and as an Entrepreneur with a tight budget, you will be doing yourself and company a disservice by only focusing on folks in the homeland.

Platforms like Upwork and Freelancer make it super easy to find and collaborate with hardworking developers from all over the world.

Go global

Not all experiences with outside developers will go as smoothly as you would expect. With globalization and the advantages of finding cheaper labor comes many challenges. Some quite inevitable.

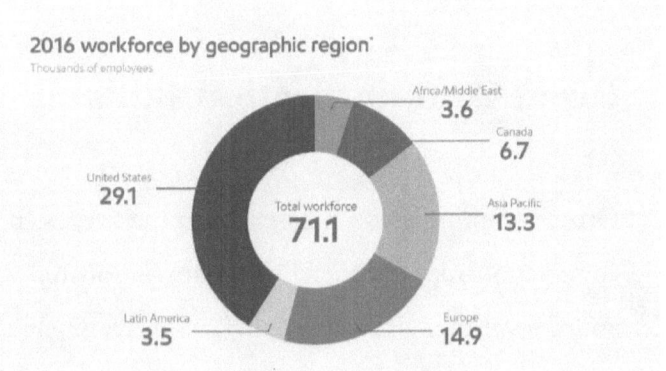

For instance, you will find that some folks, just as a consequence of their culture will have a different view of keeping schedules and the importance of making project deadlines. Others will have a hard time being direct or share difficulties with the project with you, and if you are an American or live in the States, some of these cultural differences may become a distraction.

Over my many years working with Software Developers and other types of professionals from many countries, I have come to identify some common traits that have been possessed by all people that I have worked well with.

Great Communication skills

Great communication is essential to the success of any relationship/ partnership. Your relationship with your Developer is no different. To save yourself a whole bunch of unnecessary headaches down the line, you will want to hire a developer possesses impeccable communication skills.

One who goes to great lengths to make sure that you are well informed every step of the way. I once worked with a coder who seemed to see communicating with me as an added task he was not required to fulfill. As if, communication was outside the scope of our agreement. He would take vacations, only letting me know when he returned.

Now, "Great communication" varies from culture to culture, country to country, so some of the stuff you come across, you can overlook, but make sure the essential information is being shared regardless of the socio-ethnic background of your Developer.

Flexibility with work hours

Once you have been able to find a Software Developer to help you build your SaaS platform. One that you believe you can work with if they reside in a country other than yours, then you are most likely going to have to work with someone who lives in a different time zone.

Depending on the severity of the difference in time, whether they are a few hours behind or are on the complete opposite end compared to yours, you are going to have to work around each other's schedule. Most overseas subcontractors have calibrated their sleep schedule/work hours to accommodate that of the clients they work with.

This is not a given, however. Be sure to ask your prospective developer how they plan to work a schedule that will make your life easier. Be sure to only hire a coder who will work the hours you work.

Payment terms

How much you will pay your developer for their work, how you pay them, in terms of currency and mode of cash transfer, and at what rate are three very important points to address. You want to be sure to come to a complete *unambiguous* understanding with your Developer on how the whole "Payment" thing will go down.

If you are fully capitalized, with hundreds of thousands of dollars, even millions in the bank, then this issue is not one that will present any real obstacles for you. Of course, you want to negotiate the best possible rates with your subcontractor, but price and payment terms will not be an issue for you. However, if you are like most Entrepreneurs and are looking to build your SaaS app on a tight budget, then you will want to find a Developer who has had plenty of experience working with folks like yourself.

Be on the lookout for a Developer who has the skills and talent you need to bring your vision to life but is not as expensive as other, perhaps bigger firms. A smaller Development firm or a one-man operation is more likely to come to payment terms and a price that works for you.

Marketing and the big picture

There is a big difference between simply building an app and building an app that earns money. A difference between one that no one will find out about or ever pay to use and an app that gains wide usage, enough to bring in significant revenue.

Sometimes the popularity of a software product in the marketplace has a lot to do with, not just functionality but aesthetics and ease of use. The "cool new thing" factor does help too, but that will depend on your marketing and PR strategy. All topics I will go over briefly in the next chapter.

Some Software products become very popular for reasons other than their basic functions. Take Slack, for example, the workplace communication platform just went public at an astronomical valuation. Most of my corporate friends and clients swear by this app. They say a thing like " Slack has totally revolutionized workplace communications". There have been numerous articles in the likes of Forbes and Inc. Magazine hailing Slack as the savior of intercompany chatter.

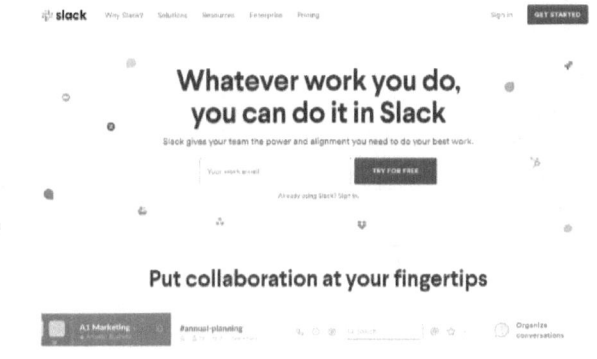

Slack-Slack gives your team the power and alignment you need to do your best work.

The thing is, apps like Asana and Skype have been around for many years doing basically the same things Slack does. The secret to the total domination slack has to do with the way the app looks, feels, and how the folks behind it have promoted it in the past. Another such app that does nothing new but has been greeted with much fanfare in is Zenefits.

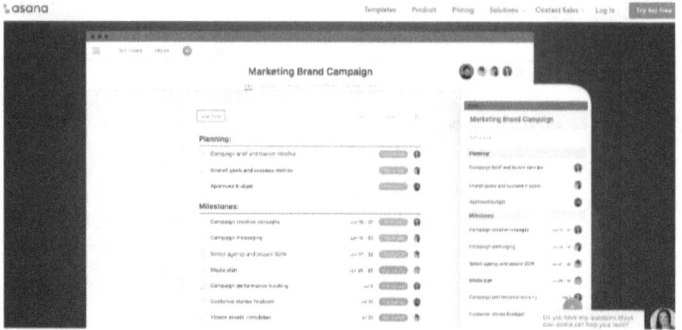

Asana -The easiest way to manage team projects and tasks

You need to think about the ultimate marketing strategy you will use to promote your app. Think about your core audience. Are they mostly women, young girls, men above 40? Looking at the big picture will help you build an app that will be loved by your user base. It is very important to find and work with a Developer who shares your "Big picture" view of things.

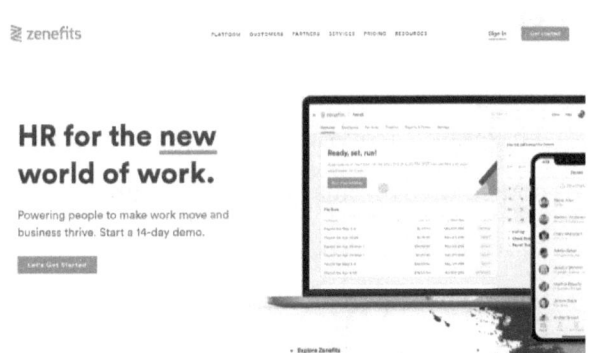

Zenefits-Powering people to make work move and business thrive.

Patient, dependable, has design skills, etc.

There are many other qualities that I have, over the course of five-plus years of building apps. have come to learn are a have to have with whomever you work with. These personal traits, I highly recommend that you do not overlook or compromise on.

Especially in anyone one or team, you bring on to help you in the development and marketing of your software product. Remember, you will be working with these folks closely for some time and you will most definitely communicate and collaborate with them often. Look for integrity in folks because they will have access to a whole host of trade secrets and personal data of yours.

Make sure your developer has the patience to deal

with the inevitable changes and missteps you are sure to have along the way. If this is your first time building an app, make sure you are working with someone who understands that and has the added skills to help guide you through the design and marketing parts of the process.

Where to look

As I mentioned earlier on in the section, there are various online platforms that will make finding a developer a breeze. Over the last ten years, many such platforms have popped up to serve the huge global need for skilled labor. However, not all platforms are created the same.

Some are built to address specific niches and needs while others offer entrepreneurs a means to find remote workers from all over the world in a host of job categories. For the purpose of this book, I have outlined a few of the sites I have used in the past. I have arranged the list from the most relevant for the purpose of finding a Software Developer to the least relevant.

Upwork

Created as a result of a merger between Elance-oDesk, Upwork is a global freelancing platform where businesses and independent professionals connect and collaborate remotely. In 2015, Elance-oDesk was rebranded as Upwork. It is based in Mountain View and San Francisco, California. The full name is Upwork Global Inc. This site is great for folks looking to hire skilled Developers from all over the world.

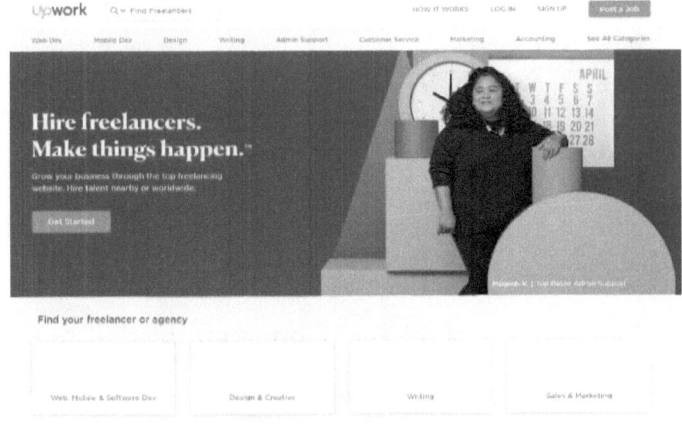

Upwork-https://www.upwork.com/

The platform comes with a host of payment and remote work monitoring tools that will allow you to keep track of your remote workforce and ensure that your application is built just as you want it and that you keep track of, and hit all set milestones. Upwork works seamlessly with PayPal, thus allowing you to manage with absolute specificity how and when you pay your Developer(s) for completed tasks.

Toptal

Based in Silicon Valley, CA, Toptal is the go-to destination for Entrepreneurs looking to hire workers specifically in the areas of software development, engineering and consulting. A privately held firm started by Breanden Beneschott, Taso Du Val, Toptal is the world largest freelance platform and maintains a fully remote workforce. I bring up this last point to say that the platform is built with a set of unique tools specifically built to help manage a remote team. Tools that will help you fully collaborate with your Developer should you choose to use Toptal

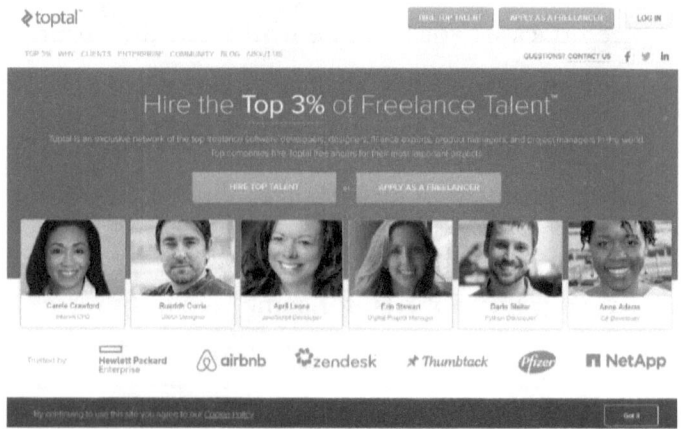

Toptal-https://www.toptal.com/

Freelancer

Located in Sydney, Australia, Freelancer is one of the oldest platforms of its kind. The global outsourcing marketplace provides Entrepreneurs like yourself and other firms with the tools needed to post open jobs.

I have had plenty of experience with this site myself. I have worked with, and still work with some awesome folks I connected with using Freelancer. Their easy-to-use mobile app makes it quite easy to manage a global workforce while on-the-go.

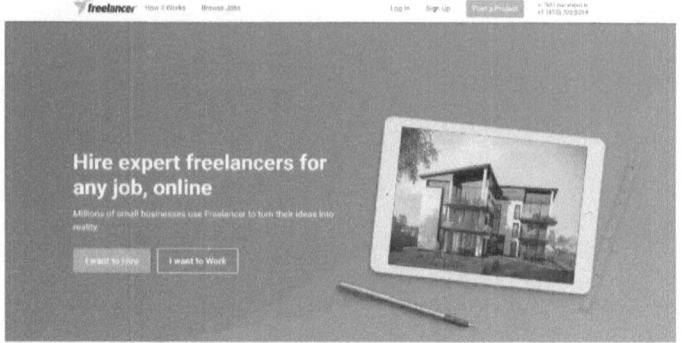

Freelancer-https://www.freelancer.com/

Gigster

Although I have not had much experience using this site, I have heard great things about it. The parent Company of Gigster is located in San Francisco, California. Gigster is the ideal platform to use if you are looking to reach an elite marketplace to find techies. The Venture-backed platform can help you locate the best of the best Software Developers to work with. You will be able to find folks who have the skills and the experience to help, not only build but guide you through the design process as well when building your app.

Gigster-https://

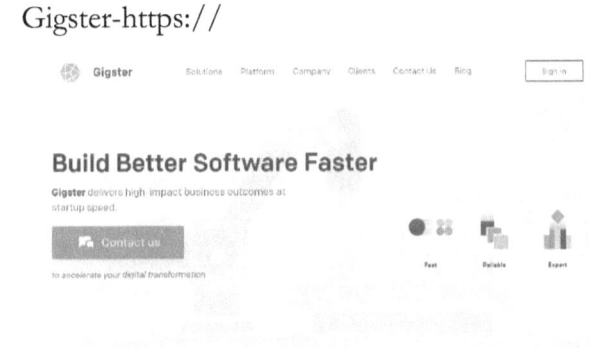

www.gigster.com/

Build-a-Beta

The Beta, the minimum viable product is a good way, and by "good" I mean inexpensive way to test out a basic version of your SaaS platform to see how the market responds to it. As I mentioned earlier in this book, it makes a whole lot more sense to first introduce a Beta to the marketplace while you work on perfecting your app.

For one, this is route will allow you to pick up some new users, who will intern provide feedback about your app. You can then use this valuable feedback to build more features, eliminate the ones that don't work and perfect the popular functions of your platform.

Rolling out a Beta version of your app, does not have to be a complicated process. In the next chapter, I will offer up some strategies and techniques I have used in the past to successfully execute Beta tests.

For now, we will focus on the core components of building an awesome Beta version of your SaaS platform. There have been various well-known SaaS products that were first introduced in very basic forms. They allowed would be users to sign up, test them out, and use the feedback collected, to introduce, newer, improved versions.

Podio, the CRM giant which was recently purchased by Citrix used this model to help build a much better product. Another app. which comes to mind in this context is Benchmark, the SaaS, email marketing application.

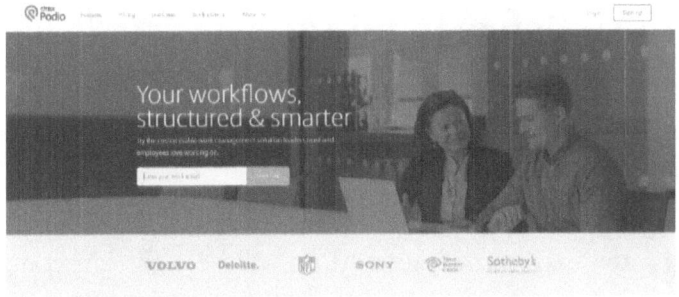

Podio-https://podio.com/

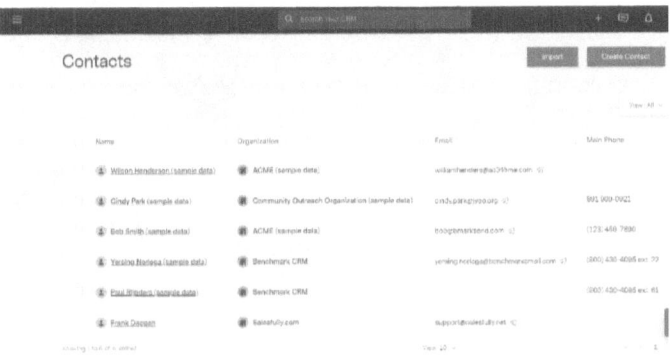

A Beta Version of Benchmark's new CRM platform

Benchmark-https://benchmarkemail.com/

Design your Beta With your Audience in mind

So, here is an aspect of building a Beta version of your app. That, depending on the type of person you are, may come naturally, or will be a foreign concept to you. In terms of an overall design concept, you are best served by making a list of all the personal attributes that define your typical user.

Will your ideal user be between a certain age? Has a certain professional background? Are they more likely to be female or male? Will your app be used as part of their business or profession? Or, will this app serve a purely non-professional purpose?

Once you can get a clear picture of who your typical user will be, then you can proceed to design the first version of your Platform with them in mind. You can determine which color schemes work best, and which buttons and text will seem more appealing to your users.

I like to, as part of my design process, check out similar apps to see which colors were used and how the market responds to the overall feel of the app. Of course, you can hire a professional designer or acquire pre-designed themes from sites like Colorlib and Evanto Market. Alternatively, your Developer can customize any theme to fit your needs, plus, this will save you a ton of money on design

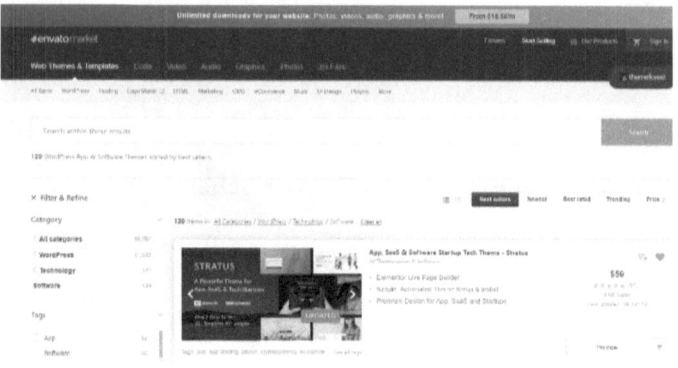

Access thousands of software design themes and templates.

Evantomarket-https://themeforest.net

Probably The Best WordPress Themes

Colorlib-https://colorlib.com

Color Schemes

Some colors and color schemes are typically associated with certain types of software applications and/or businesses. This may be an aspect of the design process that you may want to pay attention to, that is if your app will be used primarily by the business crowd.

Reds, greens and blues are commonly used when building finance and Accounting apps. You will notice that most financial firms have the color red somewhere in their logo design. Users have become used to this association.

Oranges and blacks work well when designing consulting, services, and Real estate apps. Of course, being the visionary and trendsetter that I am sure you are, you can be bold and set the color schemes that *you* want. What is more impotant, is that you put some thought into which colors you will use when building your app.

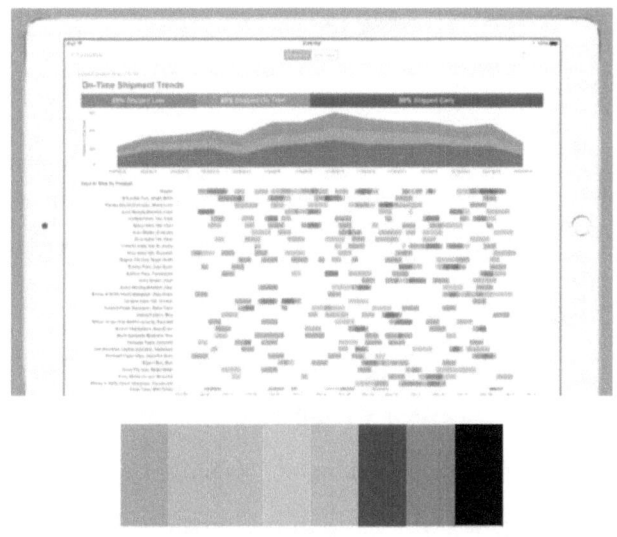

Tableau Mobile app

https://www.tableau.com/

Pricing models

One of the most important decisions you are going to have to make during this entire process will have to do with monetization. How will you make money with your app? Will you try to bring on paid customers? Will you offer a freemium model? Or perhaps you plan to sell ads on your platform? For the purpose of sticking to the theme of this book, however, we will delve into the paid subscriber model and look at the various versions out there these days.

Although, as a free-thinking Entrepreneur, you are more than welcome to employ whichever pricing model you see fit, I feel obligated to bring your attention to a few unspoken pricing rules out there as it relates to the SaaS space.

For one, business folks will straight up pay you to use your app. Especially if your platform helps them easily perform a function of their business. In other words, all businesspeople and other professionals have pain points associated with their jobs or businesses, and if your software tool helps ease any of the various pain points they may have, then they will recognize value and pay for your app. The bigger the pain and the lack of similar tools, the more they will be willing to pay for your offering.

The second rule to remember is that business clients will also pay *more* to use your app, If, in addition also helps ease a pain point directly related to their source of revenue. This is the reason why Google makes so much money, with their Google Ads Platform. There is no function more important to any business other than customer acquisition. AKA, making money.

If your app will primarily be used by consumers, and does not help perform a non-discretionary function like helping pay taxes, or speeding tickets, etc. Then you will have to get creative with your pricing strategy.

Types of SaaS Pricing Models

Like I said before, figuring how much to charge your users and which pricing strategy to us is one of the most important decisions you will make as a Tech Entrepreneur. Price your offering too high and you put yourself in a position to miss out on all the financial rewards associated with the booming SaaS space. Set your prices too low, or take the wrong approach towards pricing and you will undervalue your app.

The Software-as-a-service market is growing at a steady pace and has been over the last ten years. Consumers are becoming more comfortable with the idea of paying a small monthly or weekly fee for access to their favorite software application online. Companies large and small have transformed their businesses to the recurring revenue model.

According to the research firm, Gartner Group, the SaaS market is the largest out of the overall cloud computing space, with revenue totaling $63 plus billion during the first half of 2017. Experts expect the industry to see revenue growth of about 17 percent to about $85 in 2019.

The market shows no signs of slowing and with the global proliferation of the Internet and mobile technology, Entrepreneurs all over the world can position themselves to build strong businesses around the growing SaaS market.

Per User Pricing

This type of SaaS (Software as a Service) pricing model is popular with platforms that are typically used by teams. So, this would be for business-related platforms like CRM tools, Accounting software, Customer support apps. etc.

With this type of pricing, users pay different amounts based on the number of individuals using the platform. As ideal as this type of pricing may be, there are some drawbacks though. According to Patrick Campbell from Price Intelligently, this pricing strategy may hinder revenue growth in your SaaS company, especially if you are working with client companies where there may be multiple individual users.

Per-User pricing may prevent other folks within your client company from using your app. This model is however ideal if you will offer your product to smaller teams. Say teams of three to five.

QuickBooks Enterprise

https://quickbooks.intuit.com/

Examples

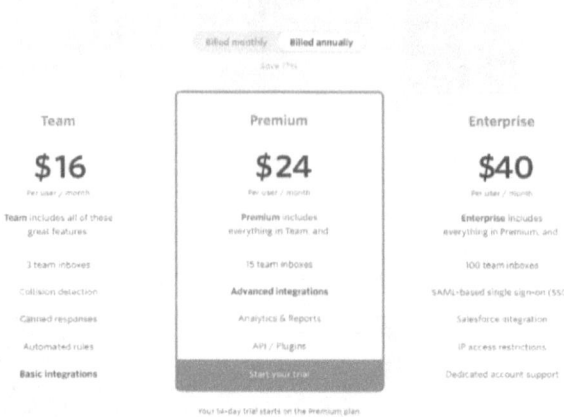

Frontapp-https://frontapp.com

Frontapp, a team-based email platform charges different prices per user based on the level features each team accesses. With the number of inboxes available increasing as the team upgrades to access more features.

Canva-https://www.canva.com/

Canva, the popular cloud graphic design platform also uses the per-user pricing model beautifully. The company has a bit of a Freemium/Per-user situation going on.

Users can access the most basic features of Canva for free and can upgrade to a single seat or add team members at a per-user/month level.

Tiered User Pricing

Quite similar to the Per-user model, Tiered User pricing strategies, however, employs a system by which the price increases are arranged in bands. So, for example, the first tier might be Five users, so in this case, there will be a price change for every five users.

Ytel, a popular call center software provider uses tiered price quite well. The main disadvantage here is that solopreneurs might shy away from such a pricing model.

This pricing model is great when you are pretty certain that your app will only be used by teams rather than single business operators.

Example

Contact Center	
Agent License	$99.00
☆ Additional Offerings ☆	
Unlimited Outbound Calling Line (per agent - Contiguous US calling)	$10.00
Phone Number	$2.50
Local SMS	$0.0075
Inbound Voice	$0.01
Toll Free Number	$5.00

Ytel-https://www.ytel.com

Although Ytel uses different pricing strategies for its various software applications, each tool has some version of the tiered pricing model. Their contact center tool, for example only allows teams of five plus members to sign up, even for their basic plan.

The cloud communications provider is focused primarily on small to midsize teams as its core customer base and their pricing models reflect this strategy clearly.

Flat Rate Pricing

As the name suggests, Flat rate pricing offers the most straightforward approach to pricing out your SaaS product. Here, the user pays a single flat rate to access your app regardless of the features used. You are going to basically charge a single fee for access.

This pricing approach is my favorite because it offers a way for folks of all income levels to access your tool. Another thing I love about this approach is the flexibility it provides. You can always add another pricing level later.

Examples

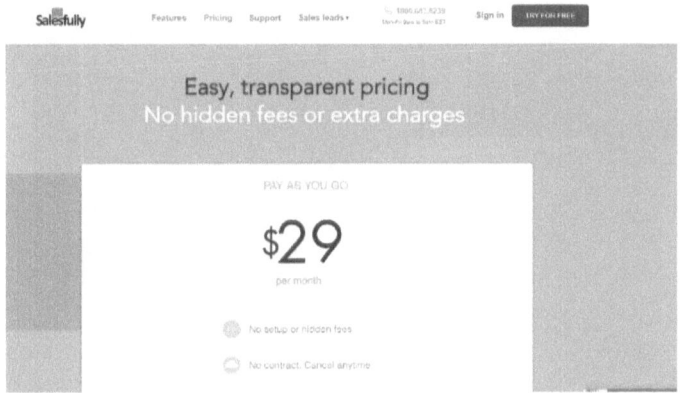

Salesfully-https://www.salesfully.com

Salesfully, the sales contact software platform offers a flat rate for all of its users. The platform, which provides unlimited access to contact information for millions of U.S businesses and consumers charges its customers a flat rate of $29/month for access to the system

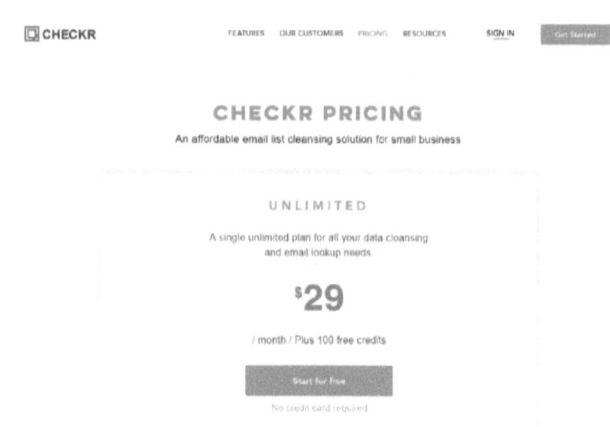

Checkr-https://www.checkr.email

With Checkr, email marketers can validate an unlimited amount of their email contacts for one flat monthly rate. For $29/month, users can upload thousands of emails and other contact information to the system.

The cloud software tool then provides details about each contact and lets the user know which email addresses and contact details seem invalid.

"Pay as You Go"

With this type of pricing model, the user is charged based on how much of the app they use. A typical example of the type of services that use this pricing type is email marketing platforms. In these cases, you, the user will pay based on how many emails you send per month.

Services like Amazon Cloud Server also uses the "Pay as You Go" pricing structure. The main advantage of this type of pricing is the affordability associated with users only paying for services used.

Examples

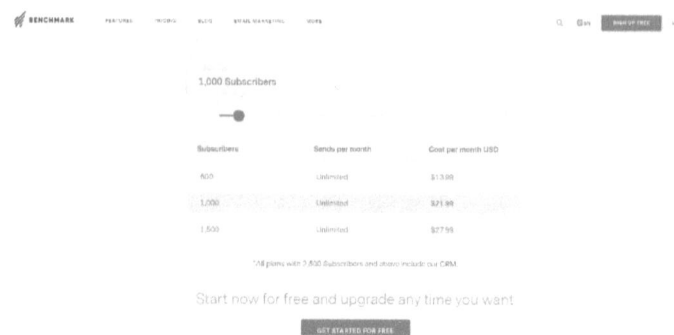

Benchmark-https://www.benchmarkemail.com

My personal go-to tool for email marketing, Benchmark employs combines the Freemium and Pay as you go pricing pretty well. Email marketers can send up to 2000 emails per month for free and pay for any emails above the 2000 mark on a price per email-sent and/or number of contract basis. There are no other recurring charges associated with using the software.

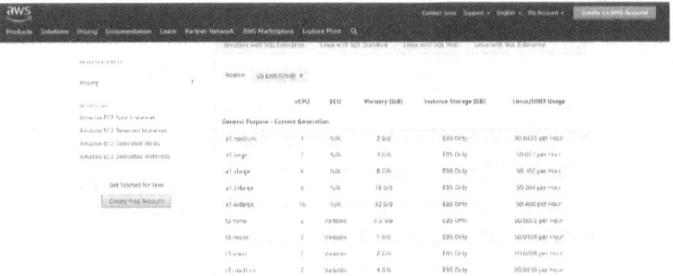

Amazon Cloud Services-https://aws.amazon.com

Amazon's slew of cloud services uses the Pay as you go method. This is one of the reasons why the E-commerce giant's cloud services are so popular among Entrepreneurs and large businesses alike.

Freemium

Most cloud software service providers these days use some version of this pricing model. The number reason is to allow more and more users a chance to test out their apps for free. The freemium SaaS pricing structure is not unlike the per storage pricing model.

Here, if you choose to, you will offer all your basic functions for free and ask that users who wish to use your "Premium" features to pay for access to those features. Platforms like LinkedIn have, for years found a way to make this type of pricing work.

Most LinkedIn users do not pay anything to access the popular business social networking platform, companies, however, can access premium tools like Human resource and lead generation tools for a price.

One major advantage of the Freemium model is that it makes it easier for folks to sign up to check out your app, thus providing you with a boatload of leads to market to.

Examples

Canva-https://www.canva.com/

Canva has the most effective Freemium model I have seen so far. Some of the best features are offered for free to users but rather than charge a flat rate to use premium features, the platform offers options for users to make one-time purchases for content such as stock photos, icons, etc. or to upgrade to a monthly plan for access to more content with the option to still buy other, I guess more premium stuff via the app.

I use Canva quite a bit myself and I love the setup. I encourage you to check out the platform to see if you can get some ideas from the way they have set up their pricing model.

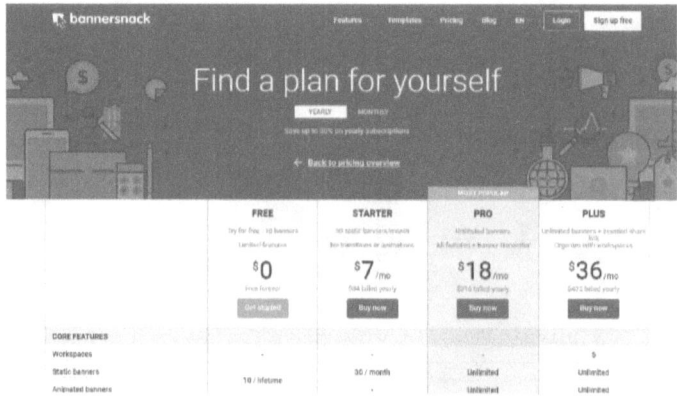

Bannersnack-https://www.bannersnack.com

Bannersnack also offers a very decent Freemium model. The Ad banner creation platform has a very effective way to allow users to see the full potential of the app while creating a pathway to upgrades for more serious users.

Ad-Supported

With the Ad supported pricing model, you offer your core features for free to your users, under the condition that they allow you to run ads as part of their user experience.

There are various Advertising networks out there like Admob and Google Ads that are well-suited for this kind of Strategy. You may also want to provide your users with the option to pay for an Ad-free experience.

The most popular Platform using this pricing that comes to mind is Spotify. The Internet radio platform can be consumed with Ads, free or without, for a small monthly fee.

Example

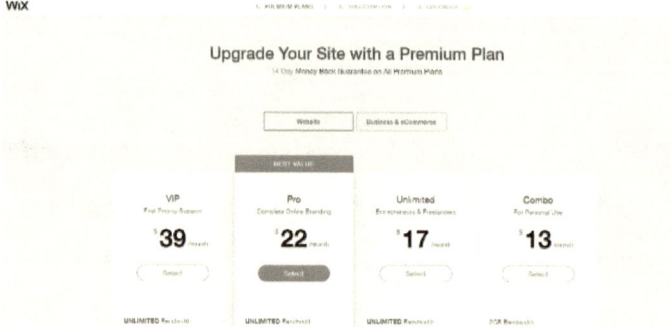

Wix-https://www.wix.com

In my view, Wix offers the most effective Ad-supported pricing structure. If you have never used the platform, you should check it out. It is a highly popular website building tool.

The parent company is an Israeli company. The app allows you to create and publish free websites with the Wix logo plated all over them, thus creating a way for the firm to earn revenue from your published content.

Serious users can, however, upgrade to a premium $17/month plan to remove all Wix branding. The Software company also earns added revenue via in-app purchases and the use of third-party apps. featured in their Wix Marketplace.

Beta Testing

Here is my personal favorite part of the entire process of building and launching a Software product. The Beta testing process is one that I thoroughly enjoy simply because I get to witness how users will respond to my product.

 I get to see what creative uses subscribers will come up with for my platform. Usually, uses I hadn't even dreamed of before. I especially love the Beta testing phase because I get real-time feedback from users. Feedback from which I am usually able to anticipate any potential issues with current features and potentially create new functions around.

Over the years, after successfully launching dozens of apps, both for my company and other firms, I have developed a few processes to Beta test all my apps. Now, keep in mind that I am not the most sophisticated person around so some of these methods may seem a bit simple, but I assure you that they work. These processes, depending on the kind of app I am rolling out will take one of two forms. I either send out compelling, value-based email messages to a relevant segment of our over 50,000 current users, in other words, I reach out to have some of our existing users test out our new app, or I go out and find folks who might be a good fit for the new app to check it out.

If you already have a business and you are building your SaaS app to compliment your existing services, then you can employ the first method. On the other hand, if you are new to the world of Software development and business as a whole, then we need to get you going on how to find new users and therefore option 2 might be best for you.

Inviting Existing customers

There are a few methods I use to compel our existing users to check out new apps we roll out. The first is the pre-launch beta testing approach. This is a pretty straightforward method. What I do is build a simple landing page for the new app. And send out carefully crafted emails to portions of our customer list asking them to try the new app.

You can simply use tools like Wix or instapage to build a simple landing page. The most important things to remember here is to clearly state what you want any potential user to do. A Call-to-action, as they call it. These should be highly visible on your page. So, "Try for free", "Start your trial now", these are all great calls to action. Also, be sure to clearly list all features that you know will be relevant to the type of visitors coming to that particular page.

You can create many of these to list different features, so you do not have to cram all features into the page. Here, for the purposes of offering a pre-launch beta invite, you want to be sure to let would-be users know that your app is still in production and they are merely signing up to be notified when the app is live.

Be sure to clearly state that you will need their feedback to improve the app and that the first version will be a Beta version riddled with bugs. Maybe not "riddled" but will have some issues. Issues you are depending on them to help you fix.

The second approach to getting folks to test your bets from your existing customer list is one that asks users to sign up to check out a live app. Again, you want to let them know how important their feedback will be to improve the app. Also, here is where you want to offer your first set of users a unique incentive to take the time out of their busy lives to participate in the rollout of your SaaS platform.

I like to offer free lifetime access to the first say, 100 users. Clearly use language that will motivate your potential users to try your app.

Finding new customers to try your app

In the next and final chapter of this book, I take a deep dive into ways you can find completely new users for your new Software app. This is if you are new to this and have no customer list, email lists, etc. I will examine various methods I have used in the past to acquire 100 percent of our current customer base.

We will look at some email marketing methods as well as some social media and Google Ads strategies and how you can combine two or more of these methods to reach your ultimate goals. I will not address any social media platform I have no experience with. That is not my jam. I only share tips and goals I have tried and have had success with.

Wix Landing pages

Most small business owners and Entrepreneurs see Wix as simply a Do-it-yourself (DIY) Web development platform, and that is how they started out. Over the past ten years, however, the Israeli-based tech firm has developed a slew of tools to help folks like you build a myriad of applications and tools to grow their businesses.

You can use Wix as a cheaper alternative to building Landing pages to help promote your app. These pages can be built quite easily and for half the cost of other platforms.

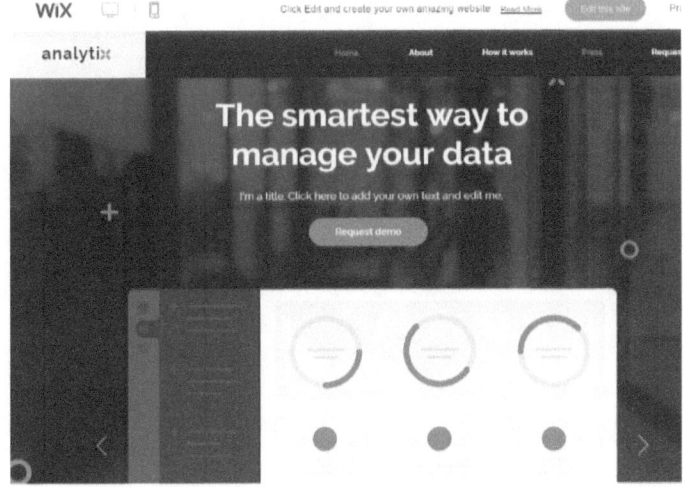

Instapage

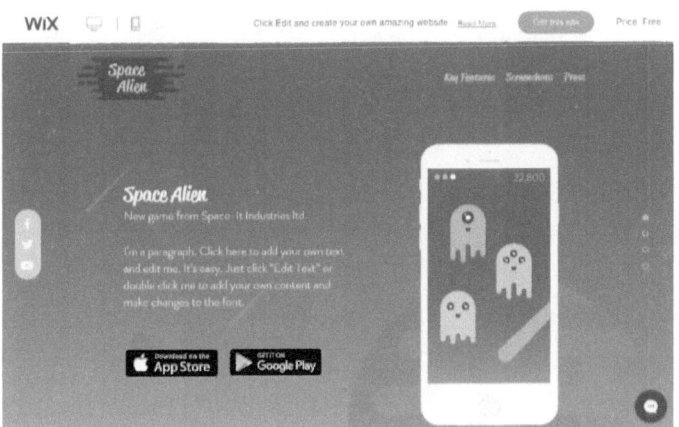

Instapage, although a bit pricier than others in the space has various premium tools to help you get the best results out of your marketing efforts. I would recommend that you move onto Instapage after you have had a little more experience building and deploying landing pages.

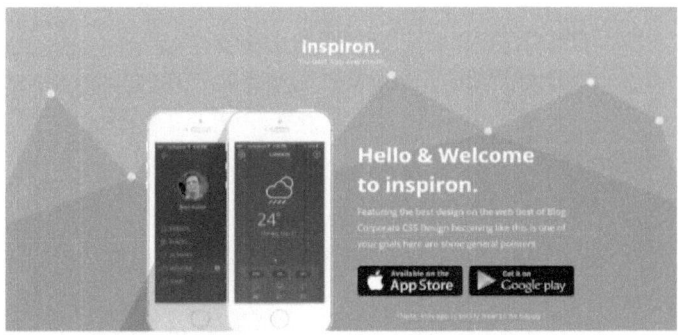

Instapage-https://www.instapage.com

Beta invitation emails

Warner Bros. Batman Arkham Beta Invite

This simple yet effective Beta Invitation from Warner Bros. Works well because it clearly lets the reader / potential user know that they are being asked to join an exclusive program.

The rewards and features are clearly laid out in a way that their core audience, gamers understand. A Beta invitation such as this one will work for you if you are creating a Software Application to which you are going to invite a segment of your customer base to check out.

> **OPEN BETA INVITE**
>
> Warner Bros. Interactive Entertainment would like to invite you to participate in an exclusive early Beta test of the next chapter from the Batman Arkham saga. Experience the intensity and trademark gameplay of the Invisible Predator mode like never before... online and with friends!
>
> Now is your chance to take down your friends as Batman, or for the first time hunt down Batman and Robin as one of Bane or Joker's elite soldiers.
>
> **What will you get to do?**
>
> - Play as both Batman and Robin.
> - Join and rank up as an Elite solider of Joker or Bane's gang.
> - Customize your Elite's loadout and look to suit your play style.
> - To turn the tide, bring in your leader and play as Joker or Bane.
>
> **When is this happening?**
>
> Batman: Arkham Origins Beta will be available from August 7, 2013 through August 14, 2013. We will be sending out updates periodically for organized play sessions.

Apple iTunes App Analytics Beta Invite

Here is another Beta test invitation email example that is great for many reasons. For one, the email is short and straight to the point. The features and benefits are laid out very clearly for the audience, in this case, app developers to clearly understand and act.

You will be successful at attracting initial users for your app if you adopt this style when writing your

Beta test invites. Clearly tell a compelling story, with bullet points, as to why your target should take their time out to test your app.

 iTunes Connect

App Analytics Beta

You're invited to sign up for the beta of App Analytics.

Be among the first to get insight into how your app is performing. You won't need any additional code or app updates, and there's no extra cost.

You'll be able to:

- See how often customers visit your app's page on the App Store
- Find out how many of your users open your app over time
- Check your app and In-App Purchase sales
- Create custom campaign links and follow the success of your marketing campaigns
- Understand which websites refer the most users

We're offering access to the App Analytics beta on a first-come, first-served basis. Sign up below and we'll send you an email as soon as it's ready for you.

CHAPTER THREE

SELL IT

Ways to market your new SaaS App

With the growing popularity of social media, worldwide accessibility of the internet and the proliferation of mobile devices and apps. There has never been a better time to find global customers for your Software product or any business for that matter for a fraction of the cost of acquisition, compared to say ten years ago.

Online advertising is now the, not only most effective, but the least expensive way to find new customers. In your case new users for your Software platform. Social media apps like Facebook and Twitter, as well as platforms like Google Ads. make it super easy to specifically target potential users based on a whole host of geographic, psychographic, and professional specifications. You can, these days market to a group of potential users based on their type of profession, gender, age group, etc. using Facebook.

I strongly recommend that, if you are looking to build a robust SaaS business around your app(s), you get dead serious about marketing. Yes, finding users within your natural market is great but to actually generate real revenue with your app, take it from me, you will need to develop a well thought out marketing plan and spend the cash to accomplish your goals.

In this section, I will briefly go over some of the main methods and strategies I have used in the past and *still* use to attract new users to my various Subscription software tools. As you may have guessed already, marketing is a huge topic that requires its own dedicated book to really break down. I realize that. For this reason, I have decided to only tackle the platforms and methods that have worked for me, just so you can quickly map out a plan based on testimony from a guy who has some experience in this arena.

Email Marketing

With any new form of marketing strategy, what you decide to use comes with advantages and disadvantages. Email marketing is no different.

Besides being the least expensive marketing medium of choice by entrepreneurs the world over, mobile technology and the mobile app world has revolutionized email marketing in ways that most people do not realize. More and more recipients of your email messages now read them on their mobile devices and through the power of instant notifications. Your potential users will read your email messages almost immediately. That is, if they like what they see pop up on their devices.

Email marketing by the numbers.

Rest assured that email marketing is not a lost art.

Yes, like any other form of marketing, there are some challenges and barriers to entry, but once you figure out how to gain new users with an effective email marketing campaign you will wonder how you ever did without it. Email marketing is the marketing backbone of my SaaS business. Email marketing is still alive and well today.

According to Digital Marketing firm Wordstream...

- Email is the third most influential source of information for B2B audiences, behind only colleague recommendations and industry-specific thought leaders.

- 86% of business professionals prefer to use email when communicating for business purposes.

- CTRs are 47% higher for B2B email campaigns than B2C email campaigns.

- 59% of B2B marketers say email is their most effective channel in terms of revenue generation.

- 56 percent of brands using emoji in their email subject lines had a higher open rate, according to a report by *Experian*.

- Tuesday is the best day of the week to send email (according to 10 email marketing studies).

- Welcome emails are incredibly effective: on average, 320% more revenue is attributed to them on a per email basis than other promotional emails.

- 80% of retail professionals indicate that email marketing is their greatest driver of customer retention (the next closest channel? Social media is identified by just 44% of those same professionals).

Advantages of Email marketing

There are many upsides to using Email as one of, if not your main avenue of communicating with your users and potential users alike. Many of these advantages I have covered briefly already. For one email is extremely cheap in terms of dollars and cents. It, email, provides a clear path of communication with your intended targets.

You also get a chance to completely control the messaging when using email to attract new customers or users. Through the power of Artificial intelligence and machine learning, you are able to fully customize each email message and make it more meaningful to each intended target.

Disadvantages of Email marketing

With many advantages come some drawbacks to using email to get the message out about your new app. The main one or ones being, the various statutory regulations and privacy hurdles constricting the free use of email for commercial purposes.

Most countries and territories have their own form of rules intended to regulate email marketing. Ones that Email service providers and Internet service providers must follow. I often hear Entrepreneurs express frustration with the use of commercial emails. You will face some issues and have to follow some rules.

You will have to do Email marketing the right way to be able to reap the full benefits of this form of marketing. You will have to follow the laws in your country, build your own organic list to be able to see how powerful email marketing can be.

Building your Email marketing list

If your SaaS application is meant to be a value-added product for your business. In other words, if you are going to market your new app to the existing customers in your current business, then you are already halfway there as far as this topic is concerned.

You probably already have a sizeable list of folks who already know your brand and are more inclined to check out any product or service you recommend.

Now, on the other hand, if you are starting out cold and really need to build an organic list of email contacts, then keep reading. I should warn you however that building an organic email list like doing any other thing organically, it takes time and will require that you spend some cash.

Personal or business contacts

One of the quickest ways to build an email list for

marketing is to collect likely leads from your existing personal or business contacts. Here what I am talking about, it requires that you first use a tool like Yesware to formally ask permission from your Gmail contacts or LinkedIn contacts to send them your Beta invitation and any other associated email message.

Yesware is a simple to use, Gmail add-on that gives you the tools to create email lists and craft email templates to be used many times over. I recommend using this tool to send out emails to groups of contacts to gauge their interest before you move to more advanced email marketing platforms like Benchmark or MailChimp.

The initial goal is to see who opens your email messages and responds to them. Then make a note of those folks. These folks are more likely to keep opening and reading your emails will be easier to transition to full-blown users of your app.

Ultimately. In your first email, you will want to be as casual as possible. Tell the folks on your contact list about your decision to jump into the world of Software and how excited you are. Let them know how important their feedback is to you and that you cannot wait for them to try your new app.

You can even start a Facebook group for folks on your contact list to share their thoughts about your app. I would limit this group only to folks on your contact list and not allow any future users to participate. Control the Initial contacts you send this content to, because sometimes, things can quickly spiral out of control. Trust me.

Yesware

Yesware - https://www.yesware.com

Track emails, access a library of tried-and-true templates, tee up personalized multi-touch Campaigns, and sync to Salesforce – all without leaving Gmail.

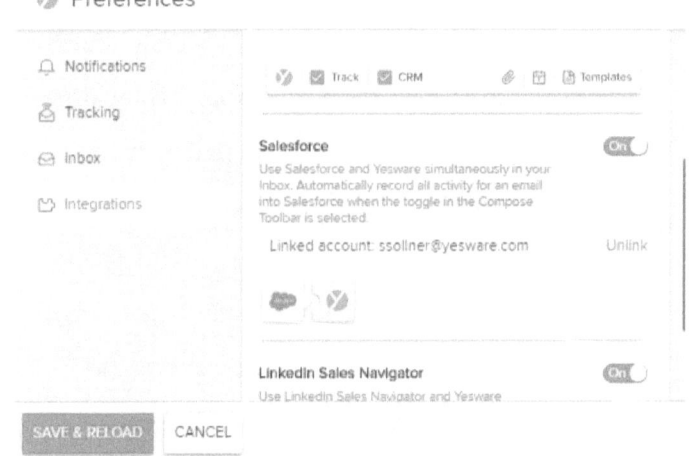

Opt-in leads

Building an Email marketing list on your own without tapping into an existing contact list is a bit trickier and more time-consuming than using your own contact list. Here you will want to think in terms of messaging and offering value.

In my Book Persona, I talk about the logic in trying to determine who your ideal customer is and crafting your value proposition and overall messaging specifically to appeal to that person. You will need to carefully create a value message statement and create compelling copy for this part.

Now, I have to let you know that I have no doubt that others much smarter than I have come up with various different ways on how to collect emails for your initial Beta invites or for any future marketing. I have no doubt there are other, even better ways to do this. As I stated before, I am only going to share with you strategies that have worked for me in the past.

That being said, you will want to create an online ad to drive folks to your related landing page to sign up. Facebook also has a paid ad platform just for this type of marketing.

Within the social media giants Ad platforms, you can build an Ad meant to collect emails from folks looking to be contacted by companies like yours. I strongly recommend that you utilize this ad tool to build a new email marketing list. The program allows you to build a solid list of potential users/customers for pennies on the dollar.

Social Media

When it comes to using Social media as a marketing channel for software applications, I have to say I have experience only within the Facebook universe. I have used Facebook extensively to successfully market various apps and services.

Facebook has built its entire advertising platform to

allow Entrepreneurs like you and small business owners to reach out to a global community of users at very affordable rates. Using Facebook to market to folks overseas is actually generally cheaper than marketing to folks in the U.S. I like to make all my apps available to folks around the world, and I recommend you do the same.

Facebook Ads Work

Launching an Ad Campaign for your SaaS app on Facebook can be a beautiful way to build a following and attract some new users. One of the great things about advertising on Facebook is the sheer affordability. Although the social media company has many different types of ads and programs, the overall cost of advertising on Facebook beats any other form of digital marketing out there with the exception of email marketing.

When it comes to Facebook advertising, I like to say

there is something for everyone. You can market to folks as far as the Middle East or as close as your neighborhood. I don't think most everyday folks understand the power and potential reach they can have with their products and services by making use of the various ad programs on Facebook.

Over the years, I have built some effective, and not so effective marketing campaigns for our software products on Facebook. I have been able to track the overall addition, in terms of new users that Facebook brings to our platforms on a monthly basis.

The average person believes that advertising on Facebook means you simply share whatever product or service you are offering with your friends and wait for them to "inbox" you and that is it.

No, ma'am, there is a whole other section of Facebook built to arm any small businesses owner with the tools needed to build and deploy really effective and robust marketing campaigns. It all starts with a Facebook Business page.

You really need a business page

Having a Facebook page for your SaaS product is always a good idea. I even recommend that you create separate business pages for all your future software products. These pages should be separate from your company page. Here is why. Social media in it of itself brings out the tribal aspects of our species.

Folks who spend a lot of time on social media are very passionate about whatever it is they are interested in. Folks like to show their interest and familiarity with brands and products. Creating a Facebook business page just for your SaaS app will allow folks to clearly identify their specific product affiliation and subsequently your brand.

Build a dedicated page for your app. Only publish and share content that is related to your Platform. So, we are talking about feature upgrades, tutorials, milestones, etc. Be sure to keep your page updated regularly. You can use tools like Hootsuite or Outpost to easily manage posts and content shared on your

Facebook business pages.

Having a Facebook business page gives you access to all the Advertising programs the Social media company offers. You can create ads for your page based on the content you share and specifically target folks in your geographical location (Zip code, city, state, region), or folks in other countries to check out your Software tool. Facebook's Ad platform also allows you to target folks based on their hobbies, professions, other similar products they use or like, and so much more.

One of the least expensive ways, I have found to build a following for your Software tool(s) on the social media platform is by taking advantage of the "Page Like" campaign/ program. This is where the folks you choose to target will be encouraged on Facebook to "Like" your business page.

This is a great way to get folks to visit your landing pages and then convert some of these visitors to users. This is a two-phase process, however. The first thing you want to do is to make sure you use captivating images to build your page. Use your profile background image to tell a story.

So, what I am saying is, make sure that any page visitors know exactly what your app does instantly and how they can benefit from what you have to offer. Clearly, show a button for folks to click to visit your Landing page.

The next step is to continue to share content on your page that progressively tells a story about what your tool is all about. This way, you will keep fans of your page engaged and as time goes on, and a good chunk will check out your app.

Outpost

Outpost-https://www.outpostsocial.com

All in one Social Media Marketing Platform Outpost makes it very easy to manage multiple social media accounts from one account.

The power of Facebook

Facebook is one of the most popular tools out there. The share percentage of online attention that the social media giant commands should cause any business owner to consider some kind of Facebook marketing strategy as part of their overall marketing plan.

The social media company, across all of its platforms and tools, attract billions of users around the world every day.

Facebook is too big to ignore

- Worldwide, there are over 2.38 billion monthly active users (MAU) as of March 31, 2019. This is an 8 percent increase in Facebook MAUs year over year. This is compared to 2.32 billion MAUs for Q4 2018. (Source: Facebook 4/24/19) Facebook is simply too big to ignore as an on-going part of your digital marketing communications program. Please note the last item on this list for the total number of people who now use Facebook, Instagram, WhatsApp, or Messenger every day on average.

- 1.56 billion people on average log onto Facebook daily and are considered daily active users (Facebook DAU) for March 2019. This represents an 8 percent increase year over year (Source: Facebook as 4/24/19). Sixty-six percent of Facebook's audience would be considered DAU versus Monthly Active Users (MAU). The Implication: A huge and vastly growing number of Facebook users are active and consistent in their visits to the site, making them a promising audience for your marketing efforts.
- There are 1.74 billion mobile active users (Mobile Facebook MAU) for December 2016

which is an increase of 21% year-over-year (Source: Facebook as of 02/01/17).

- Facebook users are 76% female (out of 100% of all females) and 66% male (out of 100% of all males). This stat is one that you really have to think about because it's comparing the percentage of all females against the percentage of all males who are on Facebook. Sorry for the confusion. To dig a little deeper, take a look at this study which does a much better job at explaining the nuances – Source: Brandwatch -

- Highest traffic occurs mid-week between 1 to 3 pm. (Source: Bit.ly blog) On another note, a Facebook post at 7pm will result in more clicks on average than posting at 8pm (Source: Forbes). Go figure.

- *How this can help you*: You have the potential to reach more consumers and drive higher traffic to your site during peak usage times, but people may be more likely to be more engaged in the evenings. This statistic may be a factor when you are planning social communication scheduling. (Also consider that Facebook has a global audience, so you may want to plan around the time zone of your key market.)

- One in five-page views in the United States occurs on Facebook. (Source: Infodocket 2012) ***How this helps you***: This is a huge market on the web; if you use social media marketing efforts on Facebook well, you could have huge returns to show for it.

- 16 Million local business pages have been created as of May 2013 which is a 100 percent increase from 8 million in June 2012. (Source: Facebook). Facebook marketing has transformed how business is conducted, and its use by local businesses to extend their markets continues to explode.

- 42% of marketers report that Facebook is critical or important to their business. (Source: State of Inbound Marketing 2012 ***The Takeaway:*** This is a crowded marketplace, but you can't afford to sit it out, because odds are fairly high that your competition is there. The key is to use Facebook marketing correctly and make sure that your efforts stand out from the crowd.

In a nutshell

According to Facebook, an estimated 2.7 billion people use Facebook, WhatsApp, Instagram, or Messenger each month and more than 2.1 billion people use at least one of the Facebook family of services every day on average.

Facebook Users Stats

(Source- https://www.statista.com)

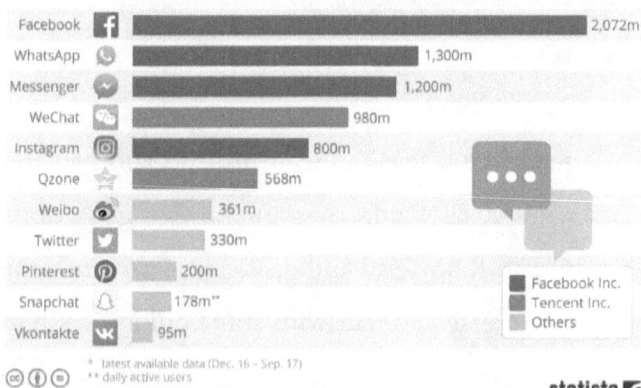

Types of Facebook Ads Plus Examples

Most Facebook ads that have a noticeable impact, share certain commonality. With the Social media world being a jungle-like atmosphere, it is hard to stand out. Users are inundated with content all day long.

A quick scroll through your updates and you are sure to witness all kinds of content. Ranging from the strange to funny, sad and disturbing. You are going to have to create your ads with some unique attributes to be able to grab and keep the attention of your intended audience.

According to e-commerce giant Shopify, there are

about six basic types of Facebook Ads. Out there, and although you can find inspiration in most of these Ad types, I will go ahead and outline the types that I have had success within the terms of marketing a software application. You can feel free to add your own twist on these basic types of Facebook campaigns to better fit your needs.

Characteristics of an effective Facebook Ad.

Before we jump in, I need you to keep in mind that no matter which type of Facebook Ad you choose, be sure to include as many of the following elements as possible within your ad. Most effective Facebook ads are built to **appeal specifically to a well-defined audience**, have **clear eye-catching relevant images**, have a **clear call to action**, and **have direct, value-driven content**.

New traffic generation ads

Retargeting is great, but unless you're driving high-quality traffic to your site, it won't be very effective. It's always a good idea to have a Facebook campaign driving potential new customers to your landing page. I call this type of campaign a first touch point ad, as it's likely the first time the person viewing the ad has heard of your company.

Example

FreshBooks

Here's an example of a traffic generation ad from FreshBooks. This is a pretty straightforward ad meant to attract non-accountants to try FreshBooks. The ad also has a clear, "Sign up" Call-to-action (CTA)

Page Like ads

Like I mentioned earlier, the page like campaign is the least expensive type of campaign you can launch on Facebook. I especially like this type of ad for other reasons besides its affordability. These "Like my page" type of ads accomplish two things at once.

They are a great way to introduce folks to your brand, and also to bring them into your community of followers or audience to whom you can continue to market to via page posts at no additional costs. You can really make an impact here with the use of well put together video ads. You can display these ads as your profile background thus catching the eye of many people without asking them to read.

Example

Promo

Promo, the small business content creation platform, in the ad below uses quality visuals and clear messaging to help build its community of Facebook followers.

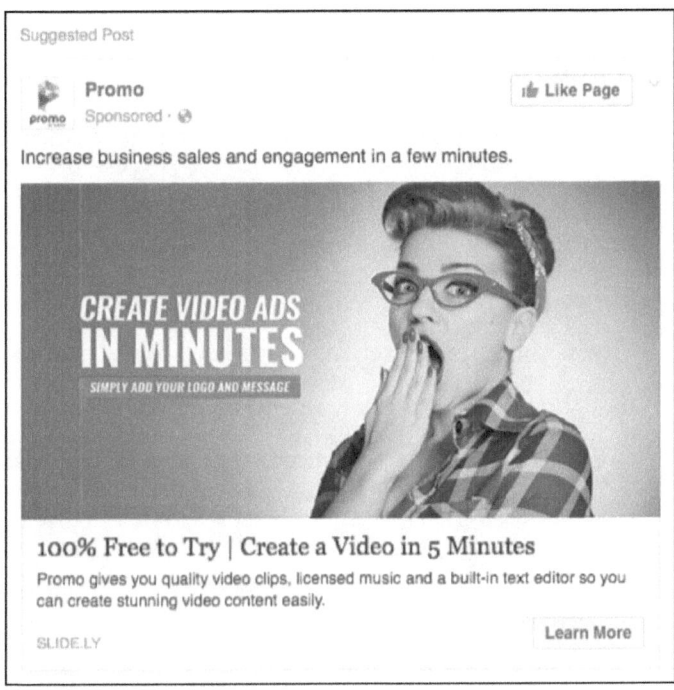

Existing customer new product/features ads

As I mentioned earlier, one of the best ways to get users for your new app is to market to your existing customers. You are more likely to get an existing customer to check out your app then new ones. The probability of making a sale from an existing customer is between 60–70%, as compared to 5-20% for new ones according to SignalMind.

What's even more amazing is that repeat customers spend an average of 33% more than new ones and 80% of your future profits will come from just 20% of your existing customers.

Given the data on repeat customers, it's a no-brainer that when you roll out your new app, the first ad you run should be an announcement targeting existing customers.

HelloFresh used this tactic to promote their new sub-brand, Green Chef. They partnered with influencers to run targeted Facebook ads to their existing customer base, announcing the latest arrival to the brand.

Example

It's a SaaS life for me

I have tried my hands at many different kinds of businesses over the course of my life. I started out when I was very young. Like any other kid, I did the "lemonade stand" thing. Well, to be more specific, a Ghanaian version of it. By age twelve, my friends and

I were running a robust event planning business. By that I mean, my friends and I threw parties.

You see, I was lucky enough to be raised by Entrepreneurs. Both my Mom and Dad, for as long as I can remember had their own business, Rexall Ltd. They were a great team. My father was the tinkerer, ideas guy type and my Mom could sell anything. As a team, they built a profitable silverware-making enterprise.

I always wanted to have a relationship with my wife someday with something similar to theirs. I hoped to find a life partner with whom I could work well with. I definitely found that in my wife. Together, we have managed to put together a thriving Software services business. One that I am very proud of.

Our ultimate goal with any product or service we rollout is to be able to realize recurring revenue in the long-term. That is the central idea on which our entire business is built. I love recurring revenue and by association, I love the SaaS space.

I have, as a result of building and rolling out many SaaS products, gained some insights and experiences. Insights I hoped to share with you when I decided to write this book. I sincerely hope that you got something out of this book. Some roadmap, or perhaps a spark, inspiration. Something you can take with you on your journey to building your very own Software-as-a-service outfit.

ABOUT THE AUTHOR

Frank Dappah is the Co-founder of Corvus Web Services (www.corvus.website). Frank is a serial entrepreneur and author of PERSONA: A Proven Step-By-Step Guide to Identifying and Attracting Profitable Customers to Your New Business

OSTRICH™
Ostrich Publishers
Made in the U.S.A
www.ostrichpress.com

RECURRING
REVENUE

A Practical guide to help you launch your very own *Software-as-a-service* business

FRANK DAPPAH

READING LIST

PERSONA: A PROVEN STEP-BY-STEP GUIDE TO IDENTIFYING AND ATTRACTING PROFITABLE CUSTOMERS TO YOUR NEW BUSINESS
BY GATHONI NJENGA

THIS IS MARKETING: YOU CAN'T BE SEEN UNTIL YOU LEARN TO SEE
BY GODIN, SETH

START WITH WHY: HOW GREAT LEADERS INSPIRE EVERYONE TO TAKE ACTION
BY SIMON SINEK

THE LEAN STARTUP: HOW TODAY'S ENTREPRENEURS USE CONTINUOUS

INNOVATION TO CREATE RADICALLY SUCCESSFUL BUSINESSES
BY ERIC RIES

VENTURE!: A SIMPLE GUIDE TO HELP YOU SURVIVE YOUR FIRST YEAR IN BUSINESS
GATHONI NJENGA

PRINCIPLES: LIFE AND WORK
BY RAY DALIO

www.ingramcontent.com/pod-product-compliance
Lightning Source LLC
Chambersburg PA
CBHW021824170526
45157CB00007B/2680